THE GREAT PH[ILOSOPHERS]

Consulting Editors
Ray Monk and Frederic Raphael

D0143567

BOOKS IN THE GREAT PHILOSOPHERS SERIES

Aristotle

Ayer

Berkeley

R.G. Collingwood

Democritus

Derrida

Descartes

Hegel

Heidegger

Hume

Kant

Locke

Marx

Neitzsche

Pascal

Plato

Popper

Bertrand Russell

Schopenhauer

Socrates

Spinoza

Turing

Voltaire

Wittgenstein

PASCAL

Ben Rogers

ROUTLEDGE
New York

Published in 1999 by
Routledge
29 West 35th Street
New York, NY 10001

First published in 1997 by
Phoenix
A Division of the Orion Publishing Group Ltd.
Orion House
5 Upper Saint Martin's Lane
London WC2H 9EA

Copyright © 1999 by Ben Rogers.
Printed in the United States of America on acid-free paper.

All rights reserved. No part of this book may be reprinted or
reproduced or utilized in any form or by any electronic, mechanical,
other means, now or hereafter invented, including photocopying
and recording or in any information storage or retrieval system,
without permission in writing from the publisher.

10 9 8 7 6 5 4 3 2 1

Library of Congress Cataloging-in-Publication Data

Rogers, Ben.
        Pascal / Ben Rogers.
          p. cm.—(The great philosophers : 22)
        Includes bibliographical references.
        ISBN 0-415-92398-0 (pbk.)
        1. Pascal, Blaise, 1623–1662. Pensées. 2. Pascal,
        Blaise, 1623–1662—Contributions of folly 3. Folly.
        I. Title. II. Series: Great Philosophers (Routledge
        (Firm)) : 22.
B1901.P43R64 1999
230'.2—dc21   99-22484
                                                  CIP

PASCAL

In Praise of Vanity

DISCARDED

INTRODUCTION

Men are so inevitably mad that not to be mad would
be to give a mad twist to madness. (412)

This essay is about Blaise Pascal's masterpiece, the
Pensées. More particularly, it is about a single aspect of
that work: namely, Pascal's (ironic) defence of popular folly
– his attempt to show that the ordinary people, uneducated
in the ways of philosophy, are not as unreasonable as
philosophers traditionally liked to claim. Pascal's argument
that 'the ordinary people are not as vain as they are said to
be', has been much neglected by his readers, at least outside
France. Yet once uncovered, it leads not only to a fuller
appreciation of the *Pensées*, but to a better understanding of
Pascal's significance as a penetrating and subversive critic of
the philosophical tradition.

PASCAL AND *THE PENSÉES*

Blaise Pascal is remembered for many reasons. He is admired as one of the leading figures of the seventeenth-century scientific revolution, whose work shows a remarkable combination of theoretical genius and practical sense. He is read as the author of a polemical masterpiece, *The Provincial Letters*, an assault on the corrupt theology and lax morals of the Jesuits and their allies in the Catholic Church. And he is remembered by Catholics (or by those not alienated by his attack on the Jesuits) as the author of a series of moving letters of spiritual guidance and the instigator of an array of charitable initiatives, including the founding of Paris's first public bus service – 'coaches at 5 sous'. First of all, however, he is identified as the author of a posthumously published collection of philosophical and religious fragments, the *Pensées*.

Born in the Auvergne in 1623, Blaise Pascal was educated by his magistrate father, Etienne, himself an accomplished mathematician, and early on showed signs of his genius. When the Pascal family moved to Paris in 1631, Pascal's father, with the young Pascal at his side, entered a circle of leading philosophers and scientists round Père Mersenne – a circle that included Gassendi, Hobbes (at this time resident in France) and more distantly Descartes (at this time resident in Holland). When he was sixteen, Pascal moved with his family to Normandy, and it was there, in

Rouen, that his scientific career took off. Working first on conic geometry, Pascal then designed and manufactured an adding machine – *la pascaline*. But it was his experiments demonstrating the existence of the vacuum, and related work on atmospheric pressure, that first established his name.

This period, though, was also important for another reason. In 1646 the entire Pascal family was won over by some local associates of Port-Royal to a very austere form of Christianity. There is no need here to go into the history of Port-Royal. It is enough to say that, since the 1630s, the convent of Port-Royal, on the outskirts of Paris, had become a centre of the French Catholic Augustinian movement. The Catholic Augustinians defined themselves as much against the optimistic views of Jesuits as they did against the opposite extreme of the Protestants, and in accordance with what they took to be the teaching of St Augustine they emphasized man's corruption and weakness and his need to find salvation in a self-abnegating love of God. When Pascal wrote in the *Pensées*, 'The true and only virtue is ... to hate ourselves, for our concupiscence makes us hateful, and to seek for a being really worthy of our love', he was giving expression to characteristically Augustinian sentiments (564).[1] At first, under the leadership of the abbé Saint-Cyran, Port-Royal was known for the particularly rigorous forms of penitence and devotion it encouraged, and the good works it promoted. But from the mid-1640s, the convent became increasingly embroiled in the quarrel caused by its refusal to condemn a book, the *Augustinus*, by the Flemish theologian Jansenius, which argued that St

3

Augustine himself had taught that all human virtue was false virtue and that an individual's salvation lay entirely in the hands of God. The 'Jansenist' dispute nearly tore the French Church apart and eventually led, in the 1660s, to the nuns loyal to Jansenism being placed under house arrest.

Pascal's new-found faith did not prevent him continuing with his scientific investigations. Moving to Paris in 1647, he continued his experiments on the vacuum. After his father died in 1651, Pascal's life seems to have taken a more worldly turn. It was during this time that he made the acquaintance of the theorists of the *honnêteté*, or gentle-manly conduct, the chevalier de Méré and Damien Mitton, and it was due to the former's interest in gambling and its mathematics that Pascal began work on probability theory. Then in the late evening of 23 November 1654, Pascal underwent an ecstatic conversion. Pascal was a severe and pent-up young man, and many factors must have contributed to this 'second conversion' – the death of his father, the decision of his beloved sister Jacqueline to become a nun in Port-Royal, his chronic ill health. But whatever its cause, it is clear that this 'night of fire' changed the course of the rest of his life. Pascal recorded the experience on a piece of parchment that was found sown into clothes on his death. The 'Memorial', as it is known, with its simple juxtaposition of words, phrases and quotations, and its explicit repudiation of the God of the philosophers in favour of the God of the Bible, gives striking expression to the fervent, Christo-centric spirituality which underlies the whole of the *Pensées*:

4

The year of grace 1654

Monday 23 November, feast of Saint Clement, Pope and Martyr, and of others in the Martyrology.

Eve of Saint Chrysogonus, Martyr and others.

From about half past ten in the evening until half past midnight.

Fire

'God of Abraham, God of Isaac, God of Jacob', not of the philosophers and scholars.

Certainty, certainty, heartfelt, joy, peace.

God of Jesus Christ.

God of Jesus Christ.

My God and your God.

'Thy God shall be my God.'

The world forgotten and everything except God.

He can only be found in the ways taught in the Gospels.

Greatness of the human soul.

'O righteous Father, the world had not known thee, but I have known thee.'

Joy, joy, joy, tears of joy.

I have cut myself off from him.

They have forsaken me, the fountain of living waters.

'My God wilt thou forsake me?'

Let me not be cut off from him forever!

'And this is life eternal, that they might know thee, the only true God, and Jesus Christ whom thou hast sent.'

Jesus Christ.

Jesus Christ.

I have cut myself off from him, shunned him, denied
him, crucified him.

Let me never be cut off from him!

He can only be kept by the ways taught in the Gospel.

Sweet and total renunciation.

Total submission to Jesus Christ and my director.

Everlasting joy in return for one day's effort on earth.

I will not forget thy word. Amen.

Pascal now put himself under the spiritual direction of
Antoine Singlin, the head of Port-Royal, and made a
number of retreats to the convent's country outpost, Port-
Royal des Champs. Here he joined the *solitaires*, a group of
well-born young men living a quasi-monastic life of pen-
ance, worship and manual labour. Asked on one visit to
help in the campaign to prevent the expulsion from the
Paris Faculty of Theology of the leading Jansenist theologian Antoine Arnauld, Pascal responded over a period of
thirteen months (1656–7) with the eighteen *Provincial
Letters*, in which he skilfully defended the Jensenists and
satirized their enemies, especially the Jesuits. In 1656
Pascal's niece, a twelve-year-old boarder at Port-Royal,
underwent a 'miraculous' cure when what was believed to
be a relic of the Crown of Thorns was placed upon an eye
ulcer. This prompted Pascal to start work on a treatise on
miracles, which seems, in time, to have developed into a
project for a full-scale apology for the Christian religion. At
some time in 1658, Pascal presented an outline of the work
to his friends at Port-Royal, but in 1659 his declining
health, perhaps attributable to cancer, prevented him from
completing the project. He died in 1662, aged thirty-nine,

leaving behind a large collection of notes and fragments, which his first editors entitled the *Pensées*.

It only takes a glance at the almost one thousand fragments included in modern editions of the *Pensées* to appreciate that they do not constitute anything like a finished apology or even a rough draft of one. Cryptic notes on politeness and on Descartes' philosophy rub shoulders with quotes from the Old Testament. Pascal, however, did arrange a portion of his notes in an order which provides some evidence of the form his apology might have taken.

In the broadest terms, Pascal's fragments fall into two groups. Pascal worked by writing notes on large sheets of paper. At some point before 1659 he began to cut the sheets up and bind them in bundles, corresponding to some twenty-eight chapters that he had projected for his apology. A table of contents, starting with 'Order', 'Vanity', 'Wretchedness' and so forth and ending with 'Conclusion', indicated both the themes of the twenty-eight chapters and the rough order in which Pascal planned to arrange them. Pascal, however, sorted only a little more than a third of the notes he had made into bundles, leaving the rest in a relatively unordered state. In modern editions these unsorted fragments are divided into over thirty unbound and, with one exception, untitled 'series', which follow the sorted fragments. Unlike the first part, this cannot be thought of as in any way an early outline of Pascal's apology; however at least some of the fragments in it can be allocated, on a more or less conjectural basis, to the different chapters of the first part, thus fleshing out the skeletal structure that the sorted fragments offer. There are, moreover, other sources which cast further light on the plan Pascal had conceived, including individual fragments referring to the structure of the work, the testimony of Pascal's contemporaries, and a work known as the *Conversation with M. de Saci*, an exchange between Pascal and his spiritual director, recorded in 1655.

PASCAL'S DIALECTIC

The first point to make, in discussing the *Pensées*, is that the progression of Pascal's argument is both subtle and obscure, so that any simple formulation is bound to be crude and tentative. It is not even clear, for instance, whether Pascal had decided on the form his apology would take. Thus some fragments strongly imply that he was going to employ letters or a dialogue, or perhaps a dialogue in a letter, a form he used to great effect in the *Provincial Letters*. But the polished terseness of other fragments has suggested to some critics that the finished work itself might have taken a fragmentary form. Anyway, any attempt to fit every fragment into a conjectural apologetic mould would serve only to impoverish Pascal's incomparable work; it is not just that some of the fragments, like those on the Jansenist dispute, clearly do not belong to the projected apology at all, but that many more that do touch on its themes, do so only indirectly, as varied and general thoughts on life, the precise place and apologetic function of which Pascal himself was unsure.

That said, reading the bundles in their original order does suggest what many individual fragments and the testimony of Pascal's contemporaries confirm: that Pascal had planned to divide his apology into two parts and that the movement from one to the other was to lead the reader from a knowledge of nature to a feeling for God. It also seems clear that, whether in the form of letters, fragments or a formal dialogue, Pascal's approach was going to be essentially dialogic. In another parallel with the *Provincial Letters*, Pascal tended to frame his argument as an exchange between an apologist or dialectician, and a worldly, leisured, sceptical interlocutor.

We have said that Pascal's ordered fragments show a progression from nature to God. Now perhaps the most common and best-known argument to travel this route is 'the argument from design'. Pascal, however, doubted if not the validity, then the usefulness of this argument, and quite explicitly rejected it and the other 'natural proofs' popular with Thomists, humanists and Jesuits. As he says of these people,

> In addressing their arguments to unbelievers, their first chapter is the proof of the existence of God from the works of nature. Their enterprise would cause me no surprise if they were addressing their arguments to the faithful, for those with living faith in their hearts can certainly see at once that everything which exists is entirely the work of the God they worship. But for those in whom this light has gone out and in whom we are trying to rekindle it, people deprived of faith and grace … ; to tell them, I say, that they have only to look at the least thing around them and they will see in it God plainly revealed; to give them no other proof of this great and weighty matter than the course of the moon and the planets; … this is giving them cause to think that the proofs of our religion are indeed feeble … This is not how Scripture speaks, with its better knowledge of

the things of God. On the contrary it says that God is a hidden God, and that since nature was corrupted he has left men to their blindness, from which they can escape only through Jesus Christ, without whom all communication with God is broken off. (781)

Instead, then, of appealing to 'the course of the moon and the planets', Pascal adopted a broadly sceptical or Pyrrhonian approach (after the ancient Greek sceptic Pyrrho) long favoured by Augustine and Augustinians, which aimed to drive man to faith in God by making him realize his own weakness, corruption and neediness. In short, the early bundles offer a 'portrait of man' which in many respects recalls Montaigne's famous denigration of man's intellectual and moral powers in his 'Apology for Raimond Sebond'. More specifically, Pascal's dialectician strives to alert his agnostic interlocutor to two elements of the human condition in general and to his – the interlocutor's – predicament in particular. First, Pascal seeks to show how no one relying on human means alone is able to understand or account for man's bewildering mixture of low qualities and great potential (bundles 2–7). Secondly, Pascal argues that, despite his evident capacity for happiness, man is naturally wretched and nothing the philosophers have been able to suggest is capable of alleviating this wretchedness (bundles 8–10).

Having thus established, in the first part of his plan, man's inability to arrive at a profane understanding of himself or to render himself happy by natural means, Pascal goes on, in a transitory group of bundles, to argue that Christianity alone of all moral or religious creeds has the capacity both to explain man's 'astonishing contradictions' – by reference to the Fall – and to render him happy – by means of Grace (bundles 11–17). These transitory bundles, in other words, represent Christianity as a solution in a double sense: it not only solves the problem of man's character, but also offers a solution to his unhappiness. Finally, in the second part of the apology proper, Pascal offers a series of historical arguments for the divine character of the Bible and the Christian religion, based chiefly on the accuracy of the Old Testament's prophecies (bundles 18–25).

First part: Wretchedness of man without God.
Second part: Happiness of man with God.
  otherwise
First part: Nature is corrupt, proved by nature itself
Second part: There is a redeemer, proved by Scripture.
(6)

It is clear, then, that at the most general level, Pascal's fragments move from a depiction of man as an unhappy enigma to the argument of the truth of a religion that can explain his character and make him happy. Pascal is sometimes described as fideist – someone who believes that religion is a matter of blind faith rather than reasoned belief. Much in particular has been made of Pascal's frequent references to the Christian Deity as a 'hidden God'. Pascal certainly believed that ultimately the truths of religion were felt as much as known, and as we have seen, he insisted that 'We know God only through Jesus Christ' (189). But it should be clear that Pascal did not reject reason. On the contrary, his fragments offer arguments for believing in the truth of the Bible and putting one's trust in God; ultimately we come to religious faith through a movement of the heart, but 'to those who do not have it, we can only give such faith through reasoning, until God gives it by moving their heart' (110). What, if anything, distinguishes Pascal from more academic apologists is that his arguments play, and play brilliantly, on the emotions as much as they do on the intellect – on our longing for self-knowledge, justice and happiness. Pascal's vertiginous evocations of the insignificance of man's place in an endless cosmos – 'The eternal silence of these infinite spaces fills me with dread' (201) – like his accounts of the arbitrariness and iniquities of earthly justice, and the hollowness of an affluent, leisured life, frittered away in meaningless pastimes, are intended to speak to his readers' hearts as well as their heads.

Something has already been said about what is, to most modern readers, the most interesting portion of the *Pensées* – the first part devoted to 'a portrait of man'. Before, however, moving on to our main theme – Pascal's paradoxical defence of popular vanity – something more needs to be said about some of the details of the *Pensées'* depiction of our nature and predicament. The most important point to make here is that Pascal did not propose simply to lead his reader through an ordinary Augustinian denigration of man. Instead he had his own characteristic method. This, in essence, was to use opposing, non-Christian schools of thought to discredit each other, while at the same time highlighting certain apparently incompatible truths, to which, it could be shown, only Christianity can do justice.

As an Augustinian, Pascal found that Scripture alerted him to what he conceived of as the two fundamental but opposing features of man's identity, his greatness and his wretchedness, and explained these by reference to the Fall: Adam's sin had caused a terrible corruption of man's nature, yet shining traces of his former innocence remained. However, Pascal observed that, without the guidance of Scripture, men invariably failed to understand themselves – from a temporal perspective, the different aspects of their nature were entirely irreconcilable. The result was that people naturally fall into warring sects, emphasizing one or other of man's contradictory characters. Some see only his low qualities, others only his great, one in essence giving expression to man's pride, the other to his concupiscence.

> Without ... divine knowledge how could men help feeling either exalted at the persistent inward sense of their past greatness or dejected at the sight of their present weakness? For unable to see the whole truth, they could not attain perfect virtue. With some regarding nature as corrupt, others as irremediable, they have been unable to avoid either pride or sloth, the twin sources of all vice, since the only alternative is to give in through cowardice or escape through pride. (208)

Conflicts in the Church, alas, offered an illustration of man's instinct to grasp one aspect of his dual character at the expense of the other. Thus Jesuits characteristically emphasized man's capacities to the exclusion of his corruption and Calvinists the reverse (733). But, of course, Pascal did not want to alienate his worldly readers by referring to these doctrinal conflicts. So instead, he develops his portrait by pointing to and drawing on the opposing views of human nature, found among profane and especially pagan thinkers. Moreover – and here we touch on the most distinctive and ingenious aspect of Pascal's argumentative technique – instead of offering an explicitly Christian treatment of the two contrasting points of view, he plays them off against each other, to the destruction of both.

Pascal's presentation of this conflict between man's pagan detractors and defenders, and the use he makes of it, changes almost from fragment to fragment. It is fairly clear though – not just from the *Pensées*, but also from the *Conversation with M. de Saci*, where Pascal discusses at some length the rival views of man found among the philosophers – that Pascal thought that the philosophical sects tended to one or another of two extremes. On the one hand, there were Stoics and dogmatists (in the *Conversation*, Pascal invokes Epictetus as a representative of this camp), who took a high view of man's potential. They not only gave a rigorous account of man's duties, but assumed that he could fulfil them; they not only declared that he had sure knowledge of nature, but that through nature he could know God. On the other hand, there were the sceptics, including Academicians and Epicureans (represented in the *Conversation* by Montaigne), who took a low view of man's potential. They underscored his ignorance of truth and justice, his physical feebleness and the weakness of his will.

If the Stoics and their allies painted man as an angel, the sceptics presented him as a beast.

Pascal's point in drawing this contrast was that the truth in each position worked to discredit the truth in the other, because man was in fact a paradoxical mixture of both base and great qualities: he was 'neither angel nor beast', although he displayed the characteristics of both (678).

Man is naturally credulous, incredulous, timid, bold. (124)

The sceptics were right to say that reason alone can assure us of nothing; they forgot that we know some things as a matter of intuition, not by reason at all (110, 131, 406). They were correct, too, in insisting on our physical vulnerability, but wrong to ignore the fact that, unlike physical matter, at least man can think.

Through space the universe grasps me and swallows me up like a speck; through thought I grasp it. (113)

The Stoics were right to argue that man 'has within him the capacity for knowing truth and being happy', but they overlooked the point that 'he possesses no truth which is either abiding or satisfactory' (119). They were correct in pointing out that men are capable of great and remarkable deeds, but mistaken to 'conclude that what one can sometimes do one can always do' (146).

Where, though, does this cunning juxtaposition of rival views of human nature leave us? What do Pascal's fragments on man's 'astonishing contradictions' establish? Well, in the first place, Pascal's analysis works to discredit all traditional philosophical schools of thought and shows that, from the point of view of natural reason, man must remain a miserable paradox.

> If he exalts himself, I humble him
> If he humbles himself, I exalt him.
> and I go on contradicting him
> Until he understands
> That he is a monster that passes all understanding. (130)

At the same time as unsettling man's faith in his natural powers, however, the analysis of man's contradictions helped establish the grounds for the 'Transition from knowledge of man to knowledge of God' (as Pascal entitled one of his bundles), in that it revealed aspects of the human condition that can be accounted for only by the Fall, and highlighted human needs that can be met only in the community of the saved. In this way Pascal's argument moves in a zig-zag fashion from one conventional position to another, each of which is shown to be partially true, partially false, until eventually the disbelieving interlocutor is brought, insensibly, to the point where he is ready to open his mind and heart to God:

> What sort of freak then is man! How novel, how monstrous, how chaotic, how paradoxical, how prodigious! Judge of all things, feeble earthworm, respository of truth, sink of doubt and error, glory and refuse of the universe!
>
> Who will unravel such a tangle? This is certainly beyond dogmatism and scepticism, beyond all human philosophy ...

Nature [in giving us convictions] confounds the sceptics and Platonists, and reason [in showing nothing is certain] confounds the dogmatists. What then will become of you, man, seeking to discover your true condition through natural reason? You cannot avoid one of these three sects nor survive in any of them.

Know then, proud man, what a paradox you are to yourself. Be humble, impotent reason!

Be silent, feeble nature! Learn that man infinitely transcends man, hear from your master your true condition, which is unknown to you.

Listen to God. (131)

THE PEOPLE AND THE PHILOSOPHERS

As fragments like the last couple quoted clearly demonstrate, the theme of man's greatness and lowliness was central to Pascal's apologetic plan. I, however, want to draw attention to the existence in the *Pensées* of another argument; one which in fact shares the same dialectical structure as Pascal's treatment of man's contradictory character, and connects with it at many points, but which is likely to be overlooked when, as generally happens, the development of the theme of man's dual character is identified as the only concern of the early bundles. In short, I want to highlight the existence of a second opposition, this time between the philosophers and the people.

A good starting point for the exploration of this theme is provided by a telling but generally neglected note among the unsorted fragments:

> *Order.* I could easily have treated this discourse in this kind of order: show the vanity of all kinds of conditions, show the vanity of ordinary lives, and then the vanity of philosophers' lives, whether sceptical or Stoic, but the order would not have been kept. (694)

Now, despite Pascal's reference to the difficulty he found in adhering to his plan, strong elements remain in the notes that have come down to us. The first part of the *Pensées* does in fact reveal a progression from an account of the vanity of the people to an account of the vanity of philosophy. And, as we might expect from the example of Pascal's treatment of man's dual character, he does not simply offer a Christian denigration of the crowd followed by one of the sages. Instead Pascal employs the truth contained in the philosophers' stance to demonstrate the folly of the people (bundles 2, 3 and 8) and then he engages in a defence of the people as a means of discrediting the philosophers (bundles 5 and 8 (again)). Thus, once again, Pascal sought to make use of the incompatible insights provided by two major profane standpoints in order to discredit both.

But before turning to the details of Pascal's treatment of the people and philosophers, something more needs to be said about the distinction itself. Pascal's understanding of the people is in fact simple enough. He meant by this category anyone, regardless of their place in the social hierarchy, who was not a philosopher; kings, merchants, peasants all belong to 'the common people'. But the other half of this distinction – the category of the philosophers – needs more careful handling. Here a problem needs to be cleared away. A major obstacle to appreciating the character or even existence of the contrast between the intellectuals and the common people is to think of the philosophical schools as opposing one another on the major questions of the human condition. Of course, there were real distinctions between the philosophical sects – between the dogmatists and the sceptics, the Stoics and the Epicureans – and these play an important role in the *Pensées*. But Pascal also identified certain assumptions which he thought were shared by philosophers of all persuasions, and which worked to set them apart from the crowd. For whatever school they belonged to, the sages took it for granted that the people were vain and foolish, and that only those of a philosophical disposition could reasonably claim to have any grasp on happiness or truth.

The philosophers' conviction that they were in every sense superior to the people found perhaps its first and most famous expression in Plato's dialogues, especially the *Republic*, with its sharp distinction between the philosophers, fit to rule in virtue of their wisdom, and the people, imprisoned in a world of illusions. The contrast also runs like a red thread through the writings of the Roman moralists. Pascal, however, did not have to look back to the Classical world; Plato's sense of superiority was alive and well among the sages of early modern Europe. The influential Stoic philosopher Justus Lipsius and the more sceptical Pierre Charron both define their versions of virtue in opposition to the attitudes of the people. 'In short', Charron wrote in his treatise *Of Wisdom* (1601), 'the vulgar gang is a wild beast, everything it believes is mere vanity … The beginning of wisdom, then, is to watch oneself closely, and resist being carried away by popular opinion.'[2] But it is Montaigne, whose *Essays* (1580–95) Pascal read extremely closely, who perhaps best exemplified the sort of position he wanted to challenge. In his chapter 'Of Democritus and Heraclitus', Montaigne distinguished between two classes of philosopher, those like Democritus who laughed at the people and those like Heraclitus who were more inclined to cry. The *Essays* themselves, despite their relatively open-minded attitude towards foreign customs and common people, are peppered with scornful and pitying references to the vulgar crowd, which one passage describes as 'a sea of ignorance, injustice and inconstancy'.[3] Descartes' philosophical system might similarly be said to have its starting place in an orthodox contempt for the presuppositions and prejudices of the multitude; as he says in the first pages of the *Discourse on Method*, 'Looking at the various undertakings and actions of mankind, there is hardly one that does not seem to me vain and useless.'[4] No wonder that the French Academy's famous dictionary of 1694 defined a philosopher precisely as someone who possessed 'a certain firmness of spirit and elevation of mind, by which he raises himself above the accidents of life and the false opinions of the world'.

THE VANITY OF THE POLITICAL ORDER

The *Pensées* offers many examples of the sort of popular vanity denigrated by the philosophers. One fragment, for instance, mocks the world's taste for art:

> How vain painting is, exciting admiration by its resemblance to things of which we do not admire the originals. (40)

Another laughs at Antony's infatuation with Cleopatra's nose:

> Vanity. The cause and effect of love. Cleopatra. (46)

Most of Pascal's examples, however, can be brought under one of two headings: they dwell on the vanity of the people's beliefs either about justice or about happiness.

The philosophical case against the political order was simple enough. It rested, essentially, on pointing out that where justice should be fixed and universal, human society offers a spectacle of Heraclitean flux: statutes vary, virtues differ, constitutions clash. This is a point that Pascal made in a long fragment in the bundle 'Vanity', which in fact very closely follows Montaigne's well-known denigration of earthly justice in the 'Apologie de Raimond Sebond':

> True equity would have enthralled all the people of the world with its splendour, and lawgivers would not have taken as their model the whims and fancies of Persians

and Germans in place of this consistent justice. We would see it planted in every country of the world, in every age, whereas what we do see is that there is nothing just or unjust but changes colour as it changes climate. Three degrees of latitude upset the whole of jurisprudence and one meridian determines what is true. Basic laws change when they have been in force only a few years ... It is a funny sort of justice whose limits are marked by a river; true on this side of the Pyrenees, false on the other. (60)

Of course, when pressed, men confess that customers do alter from one country to another, but contend that justice lies not in these but in the natural laws that they allege underlie them.

They would certainly maintain this obstinately if the reckless chance which distributed human laws had struck on just one which was universal, but the joke is that man's whims have shown such great variety that there is not one.

Larceny, incest, infanticide, parricide, everything has at some time been accounted a virtuous action. (60)

Pascal in particular, here still following Montaigne, stresses the kaleidoscopic variation in the way authority is ordered. Thus to take one of his favourite examples, in France aristocratic birth counted as a qualification for office but

The Swiss take offence if anyone calls them noble, and

prove their plebeian descent when they want to be considered eligible for high office. (50).

And this in turn points to another political absurdity: an individual's place in the social hierarchy has nothing to do with merit, but is instead determined by birth: 'When it comes to choosing a profession or a country it is fate that decides for us' (193). Another whim on the part of a founding legislator and the wealth and title of the oldest son might have been that of the youngest; born of different parents, at a different time or another place, and the relation between the greatest monarch of the world and his basest subject might have been reversed.

The philosophers' case against the political order, then, rests on underscoring the extraordinary variation in laws and constitutions, and the arbitrariness with which prerogatives and duties are distributed. As Pascal put it in one short fragment,

Justice is as much a matter of fashion as charm is. (61)

Yet Pascal's ultimate target is not the political order, but the widespread belief that it is just. The philosophers' emphasis on the madness of a justice that changes with climate is just the beginning. The real joke lies in the fact that the common crowd take the transient and capricious conventions that govern them as the embodiment of timeless, universal justice: 'they believe that truth can be found and that it resides in laws and customs' (525). In particular, they tend to respect the system of inequality into which they are born and judge it a just reflection of the natural virtue of its members. The crowd consistently confused what Pascal termed *grandeur d'établissement* (political greatness) with its natural counterpart and judged social eminence as an expression of moral worth.

In an essay that Pascal wrote towards the end of his life, advising a young nobleman on how to think about his worldly authority, *Three Discourses on the Condition of the Great* (probably 1660), Pascal opens with an analogy that neatly captures just this confusion. A castaway finds himself thrown up on a distant island whose inhabitants have lost their king. By chance he happens to resemble the lost monarch and, deciding to take advantage of his good fortune, he lets himself be anointed king. Pascal maintains that an analogous fantasy underlies the temporal order, where men assume that some among them, who have no natural title to nobility, are in fact noble:

> Do not imagine that it is any less by chance that you possess the wealth of which you are the master, than that by which that man found himself king. You have no right to it in terms of yourself and your nature, any more than he did ...
>
> You possess, you say, your wealth from your ancestors; but is it not as a result of a thousand accidents that your ancestors acquired it and that they preserved it? Do you imagine, also, that it is by some natural law that these goods have passed from your ancestors to you? ... This state of affairs is based only on the sole will of some legislators who could have had good reasons, but none of which is drawn from the natural right that you have over these things. If it had pleased them to order that these goods, after having been possessed by your fathers

during their lifetimes, should return to the state after their deaths, you would have no cause for complaint.[5]

Indeed, on Pascal's account, the only important difference between the situation of the castaway and the real world is that the castaway at least knows he is a not genuine king, while most of the world's rulers are vain enough to believe that they possess superior qualities that uniquely qualify them to rule. No wonder that, as Pascal suggests in one fragment, when philosophers like Plato and Aristotle 'wrote about politics it was as if to lay down rules for a madhouse':

> And if they pretended to treat it as something really important it was because they knew that the madmen they were talking to believed themselves to be kings and emperors. They humoured these beliefs in order to calm down their madness with as little harm as possible. (533)

To the philosophers, the people's credulity was almost incredible. They actually took the ludicrous political order into which they happened to be cast, as an object of profound respect. Yet the philosophers did not stop at drawing attention to this illusion; there was more fun to be had at the expense of the people than that. For, if the laws to which the multitude submit themselves are arbitrary, they are so only in the sense that they make no connection with true justice. There is, however, a pattern to them which, once uncovered, makes the people who respect them look vainer still. Thus everywhere the people mistake justice for something purely physical; they are, as Plato had been the first to argue, slaves of opinion and custom, and confuse spiritual essence with material accident. Montaigne developed this point at great length: 'The laws and conscience, which we say are born of nature are born of custom … And the common lore, believed all around us, and infused in our hearts with the seed of our fathers, it seems that these are general and natural.'[6] But in this respect as in others, Montaigne's analysis was in fact representative of the philosophical tradition as a whole: 'our beliefs are based much more on custom and example than on any certain knowledge', Descartes observed, although 'the assent of many voices is not a valid proof for truths'.[7]

The people, thus, naturally take age, number and location as criteria of justice. A law is reputed to be ancient, a religious creed is seen to be popular; such brute facts are reason enough to render them legitimate. A boy is said to be first born, a man is known to have been son of a queen; these physical markers alone guarantee them wealth and high office. It is, however, not only age and number that get conflated with natural right. A number of Pascal's fragments underscore the role that material splendour and especially bodily trappings play in eliciting the respect of the people. One example is furnished by the professions, who exploit the multitude's susceptibility to costume for all it is worth.

Our magistrates have shown themselves well aware of this mystery. Their red robes, the ermine in which they swaddle themselves like furry cats, the law-courts where they sit in judgement, the fleurs de lys, all this august panoply was very necessary. If physicians did not have long gowns and mules, if learned doctors did not wear square caps and robes four times too large, they would never have deceived the world, which finds such an authentic display irresistible. (44)

But it is not only lawyers and doctors who are judged worthy of respect by the common people because of the way they appear: nobility and royalty do the same. The king leaves his palace surrounded 'by guards, drums, officers and all the things which prompt automatic responses of respect'. 'Look', whispers a boy in the crowd: 'The character of divinity is stamped on his face' (25).

THE VANITY OF *DIVERTISSEMENT*

We have seen the case that Pascal adduces, with the rest of the philosophical tradition, against the folly of the crowd's political opinions. The people automatically believe that the conventions into which they are born embody universal justice, when in fact human laws are sown by chance and perpetuated by entirely corporal laws and customs. Pascal's treatment of the 'vanity of common lives', however, does not only draw on the people's fantastic political attitudes; the eighth bundle, 'Divertissement', offers the outlines of a philosophical indictment of the people's pursuit of happiness.

Ancient philosophy was itself, it is true, divided on the subject of man's true good – his *summun bonum*. 'There is no conflict between the philosophers', Montaigne had written, 'so violent as that about the question of the ultimate good for man.'[8] Pascal himself was, it seems, going to have some fun at the expense of the philosophers on this count:

For the philosophers there are 280 kinds of sovereign good. (479)

Yet despite their differences, there existed a couple of fundamental assumptions shared to a lesser or greater degree by philosophers everywhere. First, they agreed that happiness consisted in an indifference to things of this world and a mastery of the passions they provoke. (We still pay tribute to this tradition of thought when we say 'She is very philosophical about it', meaning 'She is not letting herself get upset'.) In the second place, they were united in defining this conception in terms of its oposition to the attitudes that prevailed among the crowd. For it was an obvious fact about the people that they eschewed 'interior peace' for 'external goods', and sought happiness in the sort of trifling objects and vain ambitions which, in rendering them dependent, could only make them miserable:

> *Seeking the true good.* For the ordinary run of men their good consists in fortune and external wealth or at least in diversion.
> The philosophers have shown how vain all this is and have defined it as best they could. (626)

Many of Pascal's fragments on the people's search for happiness draw attention to their tendency to occupy themselves with means rather than ends. It is not hard to understand why Pascal found this a particularly telling testimony to human folly; means, after all, are necessarily transitory. Two graphic illustrations of the case in point – both often mocked by the sages (101) – are offered by the gambler and the huntsman, neither of whom would particularly value his winnings if furnished in another way. More generally, everywhere men are occupied with combat – between animals, sportsmen, philosophers, theologians, cities or states – but care little for the result: 'Only the contest appeals to us, not the victory' (773).

Turning from men's obsession with means, to the ends

31

they do pursue, the philosopher, and Pascal along with him, points to the way in which the vulgar devote themselves to external and transitory objects that, in the long term, can never satisfy them. As the examples of the previous paragraph might suggest, Pascal tends to emphasize men's propensity for the sort of pastimes that in French are denoted by the term *divertissements*, such as games, sports, hunts, dances, plays and musical recitals:

> Vanity: gambling, hunting, visits, theatre-going, false perpetuation of one's name. (628)

> Men spend their time chasing a ball or a hare: it is the very sport of kings. (39)

Yet if, on Pascal's account, distractions of this petty type epitomize the vanity of popular attitudes towards happiness, the philosophers also argued, and Pascal's fragments with them, that even the great objects with which the multitude occupy themselves are in the last analysis vain. Men devote their time and energy to the pursuit of one vocation or another – to the making of shoes, to trade, to war or to science (35, 136) – as if these trades offered the route to happiness.

> *Diversion.* From childhood on men are made responsible for the care of their honour, their property, their friends, and even of the property and honour of their friends; they are burdened with duties, language-training and exercises, and given to understand that they can never be happy unless their health, their honour, their fortune and those of their friends are in good shape, and that it

needs only one thing to go wrong to make them unhappy. (139)

But the reality is, Pascal's fragments argue, that far from contributing to their good, these activities merely involve men in all sorts of wearisome and risky ventures. 'Here', declares the philosopher, as disdainful as ever, 'is an odd way to make them happy: what better means could one devise to make them unhappy?' (139).

'THE PEOPLE ARE NOT AS VAIN AS IS SAID'

We have seen how those early bundles of the *Pensées* contain an account of the people's vanity that was entirely congruent with the sceptics' and the Stoics' shared contempt for the vulgar crowd.

> Thus we have shown that man is vain to pay so much attention to things which do not really matter, and all these opinions have been refuted (93)

one fragment declares, summing up the common ground that Pascal has staked out with his philosophical interlocutor. But if he adopts the standpoint of the philosophers, he does so only momentarily. In accordance with Pascal's 'for and against' dialectical method, subsequent bundles turn the tables on the self-styled 'sages', and set out to refute the opinions of the philosophers by defending the reasonableness of the people.

Before turning to the detail, however, something needs to be said about the general shape of this vindication of the people. For a close study of Pascal's fragments devoted to the 'sound opinions of the people' (a number of fragments actually have this or a similar heading) reveals that Pascal offers two distinct types of justification for vulgar 'vanity'. First, he often presents seemingly vain conduct as determined by suprahuman forces, over which 'the vain' have no control. In the second place, Pascal frequently defends such conduct as the outcome of a rational choice, or at least as outwardly in conformity with a choice that a rational person would make. Moreover, most often Pascal's defence of the people tends to offer not one or other of these types of justification, but both. It seems to have been Pascal's view that men frequently have no choice but to submit to certain principles, but that the manner in which they do so can be more or less reasonable. And if it is typical of the people that, while they have to submit to forces beyond their control, they do so in the most rational manner possible, it is characteristic of the philosophers that they fail to recognize either the necessary or the rational component in the action of *le commun des hommes*.

An important example of the combined application of these two elements of justification is furnished by Pascal's analysis of risk taking. This analysis, indeed, can be said to offer a model that structures Pascal's treatment of justice and happiness in his early bundles. Philosophers and moralists had traditionally found the whole business of taking risks – especially but not only in gambling – inherently paradoxical if not positively vain. Two examples help make the point. In a fragment on the nature of risk, Pascal notes: 'St Augustine saw that we take chances at sea, in battle, etc. – but he did not see the rule of probability which proves that we ought to' (577). This rather cryptic sentence refers to Augustine's observation that men are so vain as to jeopardize things already in their possession in pursuit of things they might never attain; merchants and soldiers, for instance, willingly risked their well-being and indeed their lives in the uncertain hope of greater wealth or glory. Secondly, the philosophically minded libertine based his objection to those who devoted themselves to God on the fact that this involves a risk, God's existence being uncertain. Now Pascal's fragments invoke both these examples of risk taking, offering the outlines of a justification by reference to the two types of explanation identified above.

In the first place, and in accordance with the first type of explanation, Pascal argued that it is a brute, irresistible fact about human existence that, whatever they do, men are compelled to take risks. Augustine (here rather surprisingly representing not the greatest Father of the Church, but a philosophical critic of vulgar vanity) derided the soldier and the merchant for taking chances with their lives and property as if they had some choice in the matter, but he was wrong if he thought a life passed at home was risk-free. There are, Pascal contended, no laws or principles in this life that are absolutely certain, and therefore no endeavour the success of which is guaranteed:

> When we see the same effect always occurring, we conclude that it is necessarily so by nature, like the fact that it will dawn tomorrow etc., but nature often gives us the lie and does not obey its own rules. (660)

And if nothing is fully predictable – if 'it is not certain that we will see tomorrow' (577) – there are no grounds for criticizing the soldier and the merchant just because they choose to take risks. Likewise with religious belief. The non-believer's criticism of theism also tended to assume that there was a risk-free option, arguing that we should decline to bet on God's existence or non-existence, neither of which is sure: 'The right thing is not to wager at all' (418). In reply, however, Pascal contended that this 'no-risk' agnosticism was not an option. This was the point he was to develop in his famous 'wager', a long unclassified fragment in which Pascal sought to apply probability theory to the question of belief in God (418). God would not offer salvation to those who refused to commit themselves to his existence; either one betted on God's existence or one betted against it: 'you must wager. It is not voluntary, you are already committed' (418).

The philosophers are deeply unrealistic: men have to take risks. Nevertheless they exercise some choice over which risks they take. One of Pascal's achievements as a mathematician was precisely to demonstrate that gambling, and chance taking in general, could be given a scientific basis – that there was in fact a science of probability which enabled a rational assessment of risk. In particular – and contrary to the intuitions of the philosophers – it was often worth betting on a lesser rather than a greater certainty, at least when the possible gains from the former are themselves sufficiently great. Now where the people are concerned, this law of probability suggests that very often their conduct is, in line with the second type of justification we have singled out, perfectly rational. When St Augustine pointed to the way men embark on uncertain enterprises, the precise nature of his criticism was not altogether clear. Perhaps he meant it is vain ever to risk a certain for an uncertain outcome; in which case, Pascal replies, we have no choice in the matter. Perhaps, though, he meant to question the reasonableness of those specific risks taken by merchants and soldiers who, when confronted with the choice, forgo the risky path of staying at home for the still riskier perils of the sea or war. To this, Pascal replies that it is often rational to gamble on the less likely of two options, at least where the potential benefits are great enough: 'when we work for tomorrow and take chances we are behaving reasonably, for we ought to take chances according to the rule of probability already demonstrated' (577).

Likewise, the non-believer begins by asserting the irrationality of betting at all on God's existence, and then, once shown the irresistible necessity of the wager, doubts the rationality of betting on God's existence – God's existence is very uncertain and the enjoyments of a worldly life are fairly certain. Again employing the rules of probability, Pascal famously argues that gambling on God is indeed rational: 'This is conclusive and if men are capable of any truth this is it' (418).

IN PRAISE OF HUMAN JUSTICE

In turning to Pascal's vindication of the crowd, it needs to be stressed at the outset that Pascal never repudiates the philosophical analysis of the character of earthly laws. The people did, as the philosophers claimed, mistake the arbitrary and carnal laws that governed them for the dictates of essential justice and falsely believed that established rulers were naturally superior to the people they ruled. However, Pascal's fifth bundle (which he originally entitled 'Sanity of the People's Opinions' before changing it to 'Reasons and Effects') does seek, very much in accordance with the model of justification we have just outlined, to cast doubt on the role that the philosophers attributed to opinion in motivating the crowd's obedience. Instead, a number of fragments argue that what the sages thought could be accounted for by the faulty working of the popular imagination was in fact properly explained by force. Thus the philosophers rehearse the old shibboleths that, as Pindar put it, 'Custom is the queen and empress of the world.'[9] However, Pascal insists on an elaboration: 'opinion is like the queen of the world, but force is its tyrant' (665). Or he simply disagrees: 'Is it power that rules the world, not opinion' (554).

In arguing, in this way, that the philosophers had confused custom and opinion with duress, Pascal seems to have several points in mind. Thus one fragment, on the development of political relations, suggests that force was historically prior to opinion:

> Imagine, then, that we can see [political relations] beginning to take shape. It is quite certain that men will fight until the stronger oppresses the weaker, and there is finally one party on top. But, once this has been settled, then the masters, who do not want the war to go on, ordain that the power which is in their hands shall pass down by whatever means they like; some entrust it to popular suffrage, others to hereditary succession, etc.
>
> And that is where imagination begins to play its part. Until then pure power did it, now it is power, maintained by imagination in a certain faction, in France the nobles, in Switzerland commoners, etc. (828)

Pascal's main point, however, seems to have been that, even after force has established opinion, opinion continues to support itself by force. The philosophers were right in one respect: it was opinion – the views of the multitude – that tended to prevail in the world. But it prevailed only because the multitude were, in virtue of their number, strongest:

> *Strength.* Why do we follow the majority? Is it because they are more right? No, but they are stronger. (711)

In the last analysis, then, the views of the multitude are merely the medium; it is force that dominates the world:

> It is power that makes opinion. To be easygoing can be a fine thing according to our opinion. Why? Because

> anyone who wants to dance the tightrope will be alone,
> and I can get together a stronger body of people to say
> there is nothing fine about it. (554)

The philosophers insisted that opinion rules the world, but, as we have seen, they also ridiculed the importance that the world attaches to the physical trappings of authority. In keeping with his vindication of the people, then, Pascal also challenges this too-familiar nostrum. Once again the 'wise' failed to see that, just as laws are manifestations not of opinion but of power expressed in opinion, so a sumptuous appearance is also a manifestation of power. Montaigne had taken it as a testimony to human vanity that the people should think that a man dressed in fine clothes or attended by a large rentinue was due a special respect. And in making his case against the people, Pascal himself intended to endorse this view. As he put it in an elliptical fragment in the bundle 'Vanity', 'He has four lackeys' (19). Two fragments in the fifth bundle, however, put the other side of the argument:

> Sound opinions of the people. It is not mere vanity to be
> elegant, because it shows that a lot of people are
> working for you. Your hair shows that you have a valet, a
> perfumer, etc., band, thread, braid, etc., show ... It
> means more than superficial show or mere accoutre-
> ment to have many hands in one's service.
>
> The more hands one employs the more powerful one
> is. Elegance is a means of showing one's power. (95)

And

It is really remarkable: I am supposed not to honour a man dressed in brocade and attended by seven or eight lackeys. Why! He will have me thrashed if I do not bow to him. His clothes represent power. It is the same with a horse in fine harness compared to another. It is funny that Montaigne does not see what a difference there is, and asks in surprise why people find any. (89)

Pascal's vindication of the obedience of the crowd is startlingly elementary: the people cannot be blamed for respecting received customs and the external trappings of authority because these embody political power, and political power cannot of necessity be disobeyed:

Right, Might. It is right to follow the right, it is *necessary* to follow the mighty. (103)

The bonds securing men's mutual respect are, in general, cords of *necessity*. (828) (Emphases added)

Yet, and in line with the model provided by Pascal's analysis of risk, his fragments do not only insist in this way on the necessity of obedience. They also suggest that, while we are forced to obey political power, there are nevertheless more and less reasonable ways of conducting ourselves before this necessity. The people, for instance, rather than attempting to transform the political order, tend to co-operate with it, freely accepting the place in which the lottery of birth has cast them. Moreover, they do so from a belief in the order's basic justice. Pascal, then, seeks to justify this conduct and vindicate this belief.

Once again, Pascal's defence of the people's voluntary

obedience begins by reaffirming the point that human laws bear no essential relation to pure justice, and instead represent arbitrary customs, established and sustained by force. But then, he contends, it would be absurdly unrealistic to suppose that it could be otherwise; people are too deluded to agree on what true justice dictates – 'This is not the home of truth. It wanders unrecognised among men' (840) – and too selfish to respect it, even if they could. In the meantime, however, the laws of the state have one great advantage that the high-minded philosophers overlook: whatever the variation in their content, they all work to provide distinct principles of co-operation and a physical sanction ensuring that these principles are respected.

> Why do we follow ancient laws and opinions? Is it because they are the soundest? No, but they are unique and leave us no basis for disagreement. (711)

We touch here on the leading feature of Pascal's political theory: his intensely illusionless, starkly realistic conservatism – his simultaneous denial of the justice of the political order and his affirmation of its legitimacy. But it is important to grasp that the value of earthly laws, on Pascal's account, resides not in the mere fact of their being established. A law, for instance, which prescribed that the people should obey the most intelligent or the most virtuous among them, would only foster conflict, for no one would ever agree on whom the most intelligent or virtuous were. The beauty of the political order, however, is that it revolves around corporal not spiritual qualities. It is true that, as has been seen, the corporal qualities to which the people defer – number, retinue, costume – are often an expression of force; to that extent the people hardly need to be excused for deferring to them. But in so far as they do respect them voluntarily, these corporal qualities have the great advantage of offering a set of readily identifiable and incontestable markers upon which voluntary obedience can latch. 'Majority opinion is the best because it can be seen and is strong enough to command obedience' even if 'it is the opinion of those who are least clever' (85). Birth, too, although a purely physical attribute, offers a good principle of human justice:

> The most reasonable things in the world become the most reasonable because men are so unbalanced. What could be less reasonable than to choose as ruler of a state the eldest son of a queen? We do not choose as captain of a ship the most highly born of those aboard. Such a law would be ridiculous and unjust, but because men are, and always will be, as they are, it becomes reasonable and just, for who else could be chosen? The most virtuous and able man? That sets us straight away at daggers drawn, with everyone claiming to be the most virtuous and able. Let us then, attach this qualification to something incontrovertible. He is the king's eldest son; that is quite clear, there is no argument about it. Reason cannot do any better, because civil war is the greatest of evils. (977)

Pascal was willing to acknowledge that it would have been better if the people could admit that the laws by which they lived were not essentially just – if they could be persuaded to respect them, as he himself respected them, while recognizing their arbitrariness. But as a number of fragments suggest, even this was an absurdly idealistic hope. The fact was that the people, whether from pride or some residual goodness in them, wanted to be governed by truth and equity, and would simply rebel if they thought they were subject to an arbitrary regime. That is why, Pascal insisted, drawing on the old Platonic defence of the 'pious lie', the people must be sustained in their delusions, encouraged in their fantasies.

> One must have deeper motives and judge everything accordingly, but go on talking like an ordinary person. (91)

Montaigne was one philosopher who believed, at least on Pascal's interpretation, that the people could be told the truth about the political order and still be relied upon to respect it. Pascal, though, insisted that

> Montaigne is wrong ...
> It would ... be a good thing for us to obey laws and customs because they are laws ... : to know that there is no right and just law to be brought in, that we know nothing about it and should consequently only follow those already accepted. In this way we should never give them up. But the people are not amenable to this doctrine, and thus, believing that truth can be found and resides in laws and customs, they believe them and take their antiquity as a proof of their truth (and not just of their authority, without truth). Thus they obey them but are liable to revolt as soon as they are shown to be

worth nothing, which can happen with all laws if they are looked at from a certain point of view. (525)

Indeed, one of the reasons that Pascal was so opposed to the philosophers was that he thought that, in harping on about the vanity of established laws, they too easily provoked revolt:

The art of subversion, of revolution, is to dislodge established customs by probing down to their origins in order to show how they lack authority and justice. There must, they say, be a return to the basic and primitive laws of the state which unjust custom has abolished. There is no surer way to lose everything; nothing will be just if weighed in these scales. Yet the people readily listen to such arguments, they throw off the yoke as soon as they recognise it, and the great take the opportunity of ruining them ... That is why the wisest of legislators used to say that men must often be deceived for their own good ... The truth about the usurpation must not be made apparent; it came about originally without reason and has become reasonable. We must see that it is regarded as authentic and eternal, and its origins must be hidden if we do not want it soon to end. (60)

Fragments like this – and even more, a series of elliptical notes in the fifth bundle, in which Pascal endorses the worldly practice of 'justifying force' or dressing force up as justice (81, 85, 193) – clearly capture an important aspect of Pascal's conservatism: his conviction that political power is founded on force and that, if people are to be rendered cooperative, this foundation has to be hidden from view. It would, however, be missing out an important dimension of Pascal's argument to suggest that the achievement of human vanity was simply to reconcile men to force. On the contrary, although Pascal always insisted that in the last analysis force necessitates obedience, his defence of the political order also draws attention to the way in which the crowd's ignorance and vanity work to transform a coercive order into a voluntary, peaceful and remarkably prosperous one.

This point is best appreciated if it is presented in relation to the development of civil society. As has already been indicated, in one unsorted fragment Pascal contended that society was founded on force and that custom was introduced only in its wake (828). Earlier it was suggested that this argument represented a riposte to the sages and their view that it was custom that governed human affairs. It now needs to be seen that this argument also works to suggest a contrast between the way in which power is exercised before and after the introduction of custom. In the first epoch, power is experienced as something exploitative, but with the introduction of custom, the oppressed faction and their masters come to experience their relation as natural; men who are alike trick themselves into believing that they bear some essential relation to the positions and the trades into which they are born, and so are led to a willing collaboration in inequality. Obedience extracted at knife-point gives way to obedience rendered freely. It is true that force is no less present in a customary order than in one founded directly on naked force; indeed, as a regime gains legitimacy and wins the support of the majority, so the force at its disposal increases. At the same time, however, the great majority, who believe they are subject to justice, cease to experience the fact of force. If power augments, its exercise diminishes: 'An empire based on opinion and imagination reigns for a time, and such an empire is mild and voluntary. That of force reigns for ever', but is harsh and cruel (665).

IN PRAISE OF *DIVERTISSEMENT*

As we have seen, the eighth bundle of the *Pensées*, entitled 'Divertissement', contains the outlines of a conventional philosophical indictment of the futility of the people's search for happiness. Where contentment, the philosophers argued, is found only in a calm self-reliance, the common majority devote themselves to the feverish pursuit of frivolous and fleeting worldly pleasures.

> Man is obviously made for thinking [says the philosopher]. Therein lies all his dignity and his merit; and his whole duty is to think as he ought. Now the order of thought is to begin with ourselves, and with our author and our end.
>
> Now what does the world think about? Never about that, but about dancing, playing the lute, singing, writing verse, tilting the ring etc., and fighting, becoming king, without thinking what it means to be a king or to be a man. (620)

In turning to Pascal's defence of *divertissement*, we see that once again he accepts the substance of the philosophers' case. That is to say that instead of contesting the traditional analysis of the vanity of the people's behaviour, he seeks to draw attention to the advantages it bequeaths. According to Pascal, the sages' principal error lay in their failure to take into account the full wretchedness of the human condition and thus to appreciate the unhappiness and disquiet that self-reflection must cause. Our nature is so base, Pascal argued, our life so fragile and fleeting, our hearts so empty, in short our situation so unenviable, that the contemplation the philosophers advocate can only provoke a host of tormenting passions that Pascal encapsulates in the term 'ennui':

> *Ennui.* Man finds nothing so intolerable as to be in a state of complete rest, without passions, without occupation, without diversion, without effort.
>
> Then he faces his nullity, loneliness, inadequacy, dependence, helplessness, emptiness.
>
> And at once there wells up from the depths of his soul boredom, gloom, depression, chagrin, resentment, despair. (622)

The sages, in other words, complain that the activities that the people pursue are trivial and distracting, and rule out all opportunity for reflection; Pascal responds that that is indeed exactly their point.

Early on we saw that the sages dwelt in particular on the ridiculous way in which the people devoted themselves to procuring objects that they would not accept if offered. However, Pascal insists, if men prefer means to ends, it is because the attainment of a goal implies rest, while its pursuit involves agitation and distraction. As Pascal puts it in the longest fragment in the bundle 'Divertissement':

> That is all that men have been able to devise for attaining happiness; those who philosophise about it, holding that people are quite unreasonable to spend all

day chasing a hare they would not have wanted to buy, have little knowledge of our nature. The hare itself would not save us from thinking about death and the miseries distracting us, but hunting does so. (136)

And as with hunting so with gambling: it is the distraction of the suspense, not the prize, that men are after (136). As a mathematician, Pascal demonstrated that it was, under certain definable conditions, rational to gamble. As a moralist – or an anti-moralist – he defended the rationality of the pastime of gambling.

Just as Pascal's account of the horrors of self-reflection offers a new perspective on popular pastimes, so it offers one on the advantages of social pre-eminence. Traditionally the philosophers had criticized the vulgar belief that wealth and status were desirable things – they do not spare men any of the main afflictions of the human condition and involve all sorts of additional cares and dangers. As Pascal had put it in a fragment in the bundle 'Vanity':

That something so obvious as the vanity of the world should be so little recognised that people find it odd and surprising to be told that it is foolish to seek greatness; that is most remarkable. (16)

A number of fragments in the bundle 'Divertissement', however, put the other side of the case, and point to the many opportunities for frivolous diversions that high rank offers:

That, in fact, is the main joy of being a king, because people are continually trying to divert him and procure him every kind of pleasure. A king is surrounded by people whose only thought is to divert him and stop him thinking about himself, because, king though he is, he becomes unhappy as soon as he thinks about himself. (136)

So much for the happiness found in pastimes. On Pascal's account, however, the greater concerns with which men occupy themselves play a similarly distracting role. This, of course, is true of all the cares and responsibilities that we impose on ourselves from the learning of languages to the execution of religious duties (139). However, from the point of view of the sages, men's investment in their social position and occupation provided a particularly striking example of popular vanity. The philosophers, here betraying their privileged, leisured backgrounds, held that one should have no trade, or at least that it should be subordinate to the cultivation of self-knowledge and inner-peace, yet the people dedicated themselves to their occupations as if they were the most important thing in the world. The pedant, with his obsession with his own specialism, provides one particularly striking example (587), but 'Vanity is so firmly anchored in man's heart that a soldier, a rough, a cook or a porter, will boast and expect admirers' (627). Pascal, of course, agrees with the philosophers about the essential point:

Without examining every particular kind of occupation it is sufficient to put them all under the heading of diversion. (478)

But his conclusion differs from theirs: by devoting themselves to the social roles in which chance has cast them, men effectively find some consolation for their nothingness and a shield from *ennui*.

Finally, by way of conclusion, it can be shown that, just as men's identification with their arbitrarily allotted social and political roles works as an escapist diversion that renders them happy, so obversely, men's addiction to *divertissement* renders them sociable and thus contributes to earthly peace and justice. In their eagerness to distract themselves, men willingly submerge themselves in the roles into which fortune has cast them: they bear the perilous burdens of leadership, the wearisome duties of subservience, the dangers associated with war or the drudgery of domestic labour. In this way, Pascal's defence of the crowd's views about justice and his defence of its opinions about happiness converge.

We are, at last, in a position to get the full measure of the errors at the heart of the philosophical tradition. The sages insisted that the common people were entirely governed by concupiscence, and Pascal's analysis points to the same conclusion or, more particularly, it suggests they are governed by force and concupiscence. Their mistake, however, was to have failed to appreciate the extraordinary way in which men had turned their corruption back on itself; cupidity and violence, apparently the most anti-social principles imaginable, in fact engender their own peaceful and happy order. It is this achievement to which Pascal alluded when he wrote in one fragment:

We have established and developed out of concupiscence admirable rules of polity, ethics and justice, but at
root, the evil root of man, this evil stuff of which we are
made is only concealed; it is not pulled up. (211)

'A CONSTANT SWING, FROM PRO TO CON'

No simple formulation will do justice to all that Pascal's encomium to human vanity was intended to achieve. It is clear, though, that Pascal's vindication of vulgar conduct did not represent the end of his argument. Pascal was doubtless especially keen to discredit the philosophers and thus to emphasize the sense in the conduct of the people; after all, his apology was intended to be addressed to philosophically-minded readers and it was these he wanted to confound. He thought he could detect in the philosophical tradition as a whole, even among the self-styled 'sceptics', a conceited intellectualism – a utopian rationalism – which he was determined to shake and unsettle. But he continued to maintain that the philosopher's case against popular vanity was valid, and thus in turn discredited the people:

Constant swing from pro to con.

Thus we have shown that man is vain to pay so much attention to things which do not really matter, and all these opinions have been refuted.

Then we have showed that all these opinions are perfectly sound, so that, all these examples of vanity being perfectly justified, ordinary people are not as vain as they are said to be. Thus we refuted the opinion which refuted that of the people.

But we must now refute this last proposition and show

that it is still true that the people are vain, although their opinions are sound, because they do not see the truth when it is there, and assume things to be true when they are not, with the result that their opinions are always thoroughly wrong and unsound. (93)

Thus Pascal's juxtaposition of the attitudes of the 'wise' and the 'ignorant' conforms to the dialectic sketched earlier. That is to say, Pascal's analysis presents the attitudes of the sages and those of the people as two opposing errors, like those of the Stoics and the sceptics regarding human nature. Now, as in the case of that opposition, the one between the philosophers and the people works first and foremost to negative effect: Pascal uses the two worldly systems of thought to undermine each other, thus contributing to his portrait of human ignorance and wretchedness – to the argument that 'man without faith can know neither true good nor justice' (148). But Pascal's analysis does not only have this negative import. In the first place, Pascal unexpectedly invokes his defence of the people twice in the bundle 'Greatness' as evidence of man's nobility:

Greatness. Causes and effects show the greatness of man in producing such excellent order from his concupiscence. (106)

And

Man's greatness even in his concupiscence. He has managed to produce such a remarkable system from it and make it the image of true charity. (118)

Moreover, Pascal's arguments do not just contribute in this way to both parts of his portrait of man's enigmatic combination of lowliness and grandeur; they also work to raise a host of questions that it can be shown Christianity alone can answer. As the apology progressed, its reader was to learn that the Christian religion could explain man's ignorance of justice and his unhappiness by reference to the Fall; could make them bearable by presenting them as a just punishment for man's sins; and was able to offer, in the community of the saved, a realm of pure justice, and a source of genuine, lasting happiness infinitely superior to anything found on earth. In other words, Pascal's defence of the people – his insistence on the sanity in human vanity – represents just one turn on the long and winding road towards the knowledge and love of God through Jesus Christ. As turns go, though, it is unusually suggestive.

NOTES

1. All translations of the *Pensées* are taken from Alban Krailsheimer's Penguin edition (Harmondsworth, 1966). Krailsheimer follows Louis Lafuma's standard French arrangement (Editions de Seuil, 1962), itself based on the so-called 'First Copy'. Numbers in brackets refer, then, to both Krailsheimer's and Lafuma's ordering.

2. Pierre Charron, *De la sagesse*, ed. Barbra Negroni (Fayard, Paris, 1986), pp. 337–8. More specifically, *Of Wisdom* offers a 'portrait of man' which distinguishes between five qualities common to 'the common crowd': vanity, weakness, inconstancy, wretchedness and pride. These resemble and quite possibly provide a source for the headings of Pascal's early bundles, 'Vanity', 'Wretchedness' and 'Boredom', in which he lays out the case against the people.

3. Michel de Montaigne, *Essais*, ed. A Micha, 3 vols (Garnier-Flammarion, Paris, 1969), vol. II, p. 288.

4. René Descartes, *Discourse on the Method*, trans. F. E. Sutcliffe (Penguin, London, 1968), p. 28.

5. *Three Discourses on the Condition of the Great, Pascal, Selections*, ed. and trans. Richard H. Popkin (Macmillan, New York, 1989), p. 74–5.

6. *Essais*, vol. I, p. 162.

7. *Discourse on the Method*, p. 39.

8. *Essais*, vol. II, p. 243.

9. *Essais*, vol. I, p. 162.

DATE DUE

DEC 18 2006			
DEC 11 REC'D			
		DISCARDED	
GAYLORD			PRINTED IN U.S.A.

B 1901 .P43 R64 1999

Rogers, Ben.

Pascal

$6.00

THE MORALIST who advocated dressing up, the ascetic who liked a flutter, the devout Christian who lauded vanity, Pascal is a funnier, more ironic philosopher than his reputation as an anguished existentialist would suggest.

Yet however irreverent the terms of his ironic project, its underlying impetus is both serious and profound. In this superb new introduction to the thinker and his thought, Ben Rogers demonstrates the deep wisdom of Pascal's defense of popular folly—a defense which he used to highlight the higher delusions of the learned.

Setting the *Pensées* in the context of Pascal's life and philosophical career, Rogers reveals how their apparent frivolity underpins a fascinating far-reaching and still challenging body of moral and political thought. His remarkable guide offers an eye-opening account of the work of a marvelous and much neglected thinker.

BEN ROGERS wrote a doctorate at Oxford on the moral and political thought of Pascal and his associates. He reviews regularly for the *Independent on Sunday* and other papers, a working on a biography of A. J. Ayer.

CONSULTING EDITORS: Ray Monk and Frederic Raphael

ROUTLEDGE

29 WEST 35TH STREET
NEW YORK, NY 10001
WWW.ROUTLEDGE-NY.COM

ISBN 0-415-92398-0

9 780415 923989

Front cover image courtesy of Archive Photos
Front cover design by Big Fish, San Francisco

O9-ATZ-461